AMICUS ILLUSTRATED • AMICUS INK

DO YOU REALLY WANT TO MEET A CHEETAH?

WRITTEN BY CARI MEISTER   ILLUSTRATED BY DANIELE FABBRI

Amicus Illustrated and Amicus Ink
are published by Amicus
P.O. Box 1329
Mankato, MN 56002
www.amicuspublishing.us

Library of Congress Cataloging-in-Publication Data
Names: Meister, Cari, author. | Fabbri, Daniele, 1978–
    illustrator.
Title: Do you really want to meet a cheetah? / by Cari
    Meister ; illustrated by Daniele Fabbri.
Description: Mankato, Minnesota : Amicus Illustrated/
    Amicus Ink, [2019] | Series: Do you really want to
    meet...? | Audience: K to grade 3.
Identifiers: LCCN 2017039250 (print) | LCCN
    2017052842 (ebook) | ISBN 9781681514727 (pdf)
    | ISBN 9781681513904 (library binding) | ISBN
    9781681523101 (pbk.)
Subjects: LCSH: Cheetah–Juvenile literature. | Safaris–
    Juvenile literature.
Classification: LCC QL737.C23 (ebook) | LCC QL737.
    C23 M4535 2019 (print) | DDC 599.75/9–dc23
LC record available at https://lccn.loc.gov/2017039250

Editor: Rebecca Glaser
Designer: Kathleen Petelinsek

Printed in the United States of America

HC 10 9 8 7 6 5 4 3 2 1
PB 10 9 8 7 6 5 4 3 2 1

ABOUT THE AUTHOR

Cari Meister has written more than 200 books for children,
including the TINY series (Viking), and the FAIRY HILL
series (Scholastic). She lives in Edwards, Colorado with
her husband, four sons, a goldendoodle named Koki, and
an Arabian horse named Sir William. Find out more at
carimeister.com.

ABOUT THE ILLUSTRATOR

Daniele Fabbri was born in Ravenna, Italy, in 1978. He
graduated from Istituto Europeo di Design in Milan, Italy,
and started his career as a cartoon animator, storyboarder,
and background designer for animated series. He has
worked as a freelance illustrator since 2003, collaborating
with advertising agencies and international publishers, and
has illustrated many books for Amicus.

What's the fastest land animal?
No. It's not you.

It's a cheetah! A cheetah can go from 0 to 60 mph (96.6 km/h) in three seconds! Why can't you go that fast? Well, to start . . .

. . . you don't have a tail. A cheetah's tail helps it balance and steer at high speeds. And you don't have claws. A cheetah's claws grip the ground as it runs.

What's that? You want to meet a cheetah? Most cheetahs live in Africa. That's halfway around the world. It would be a really long flight! Do you still *really* want to meet a cheetah? Okay! It's safari time!

There's a cheetah cub!
Why is he at the airport?
He's with a conservation worker.
She's raising awareness about
cheetahs, because they are
at risk of dying out.

Isn't the cub cute? He has a fluffy mantle of fur on his back. It helps him hide in tall grass so that predators can't find him. But this cub can't live in the wild anymore. His mother was killed.

The safari guide will take you to camp. In the morning, you can start looking for cheetahs. Like other big cats, cheetahs are carnivores. But *unlike* other big cats, cheetahs are diurnal. They hunt during the day.

Good morning! Let's go explore the savanna—these grasslands are a cheetah's natural habitat. Do you see the impala? Cheetahs often hunt small antelopes like the impala—so a cheetah may be near.

Look, there's one on that termite mound!
Cheetahs have excellent eyesight. They
perch on tall termite mounds to look for prey.

Maybe we can see a cheetah even closer. Let's keep looking. Hold on, this is a bumpy ride! Watch out for the zebra! Whoa! That was close.

THUMP! SCRATCH! What's that?

A cheetah jumped on the roof! Stay calm. She doesn't seem interested in you. She is searching for prey. Oh! She sees something!

It's a warthog! The cheetah takes off running.
The warthog doesn't stand a chance.

The cheetah grabs his back. Then she sinks her
teeth into his neck. She'll have a good meal today.

Wow! That was amazing! What other wild animals will you see on the savanna? Be on the lookout! What can you find?

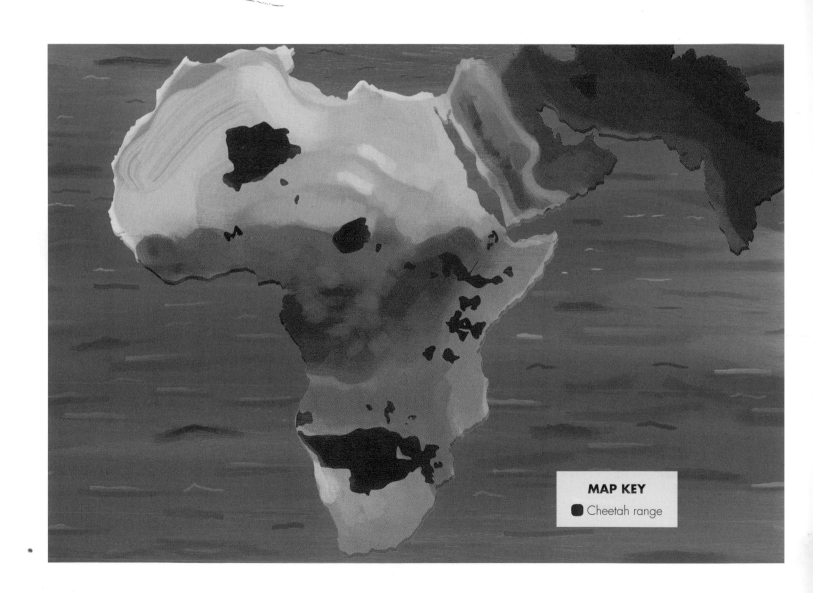

MAP KEY

● Cheetah range

GLOSSARY

carnivore An animal that eats meat.

conservation worker A person who tries to protect animals from dying out.

diurnal Active during the day.

impala A medium-sized African antelope.

mantle Fluffy hair down the back of a cheetah cub; it disappears as the cub grows.

predator An animal that hunts other animals for food.

prey An animal that is hunted for food.

savanna A flat, grassy plain with few trees.

warthog A wild pig with a long snout and four tusks.

READ MORE

Gillespie, Katie. Meet the Cheetah. New York: Smartbook Media Inc., 2017.

Herrington, Lisa M. **Cheetahs and Leopards**. New York: Children's Press, 2016.

Leaf, Christina. **Baby Cheetahs**. Minneapolis: Bellwether Media, 2015.

WEBSITES

Cheetah Conservation Fund
http://cheetah.org/about-the-cheetah/for-kids/
Learn what you can do to help save cheetahs from extinction.

National Geographic Kids: Cheetah
https://kids.nationalgeographic.com/animals/cheetah/
Watch a video of the world's fastest land animal and play educational games.

San Diego Zoo Kids
http://kids.sandiegozoo.org/animals/african-cheetah
Look at photos of cheetahs and learn some interesting facts.

Every effort has been made to ensure that these websites are appropriate for children. However, because of the nature of the Internet, it is impossible to guarantee that these sites will remain active indefinitely or that their contents will not be altered.